The EVERYBODY POOPS Coloring Book

FOR MASTER POOPERS!

Justine Avery **Olga Zhuravlova**

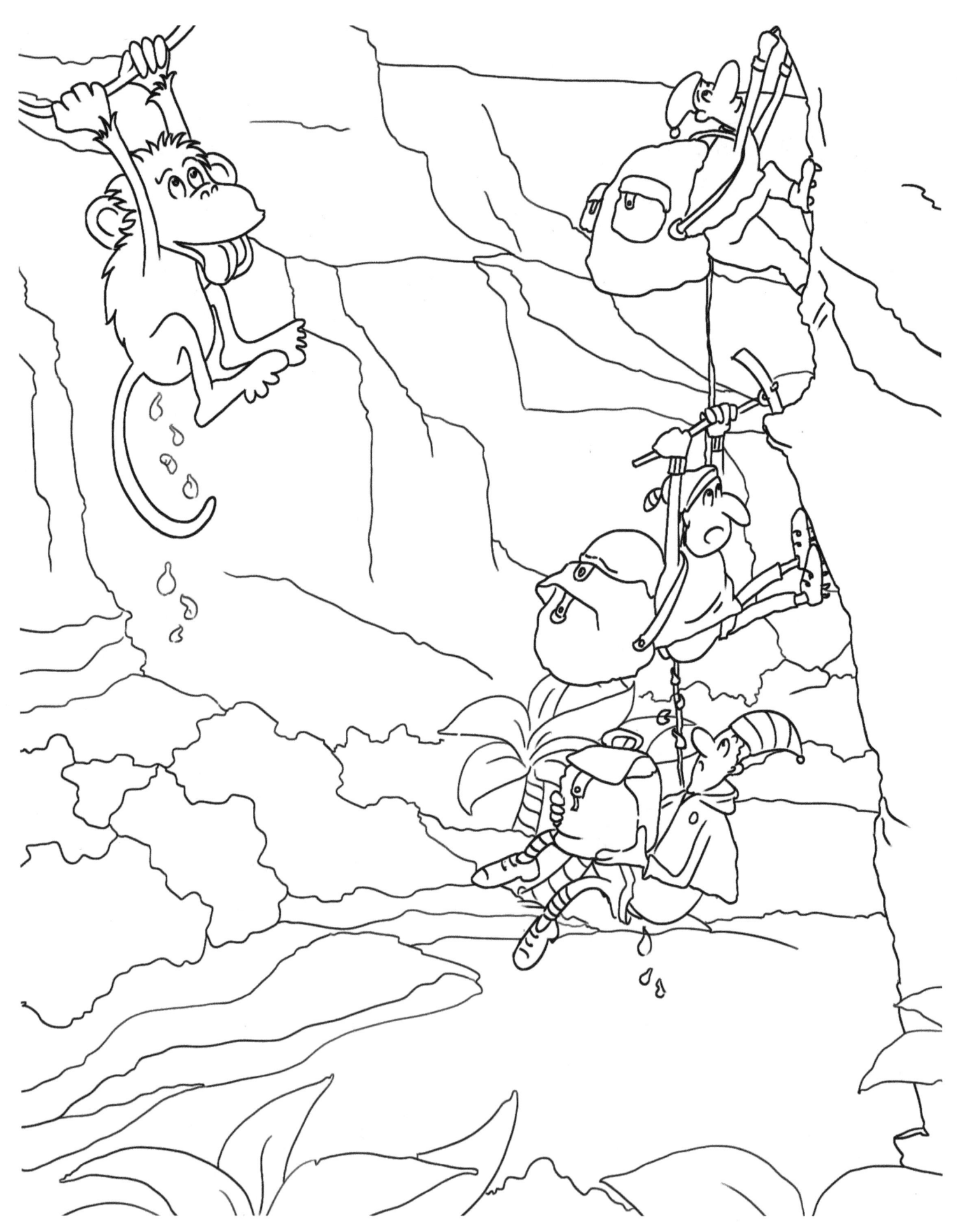

More read-along, color-in, giggle-all-day-long Coloring & Activity Books from Suteki Creative!

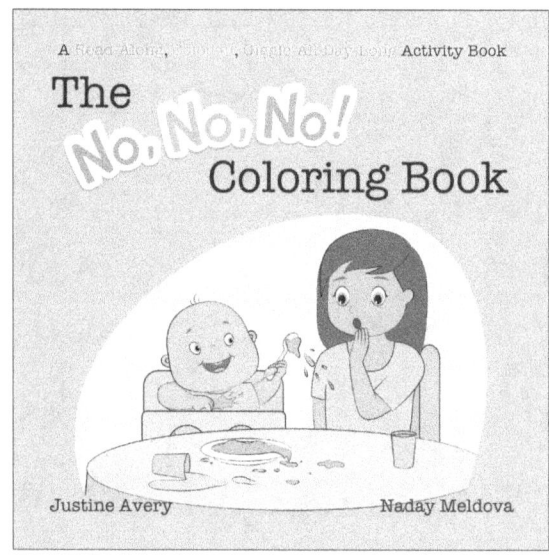

Discover more...

uniquely wonderful, utterly imaginative children's books by Justine Avery.

JOIN IN THE FUN!

Visit JustineAvery.com, and join in all the exclusive fun and freebies.

www.ingramcontent.com/pod-product-compliance
Lightning Source LLC
LaVergne TN
LVHW081530060526
838200LV00049B/2276